Flute & Guitar:

Duets for Any Occasion

By Mark Hanson

Published by:

ACCENT ON MUSIC
PMB#252, 19363 Willamette Dr.
West Linn, OR 97068 USA
E-Mail: info@AccentOnMusic.com
Website: www.AccentOnMusic.com

Unless otherwise notated, all contents, including cover artwork, Copyright © 2001 Accent On Music, Mark D. Hanson and Greta M. Pedersen.
Author photo of Mark Hanson by Mike Huibregtse.

First Printing 2001 - 10 9 8 7 6 5 4 3 2
Printed in the United States of America.

Library of Congress Catalogue in Publication Data
Hanson, Mark D. 1951-
Flute & Guitar: Duets for Any Occasion
1. Guitar—Methods—Self-Instruction. I. Title.
Paperback with CD

Introduction

Welcome to *Flute & Guitar: Duets for Any Occasion*. Our goal with this book and recording is to provide a wide-ranging selection of high-quality music to flautists and guitarists. The music can be played live by two players, or by one individual using the recording as a duet "partner". Other C instruments, like violin or oboe, can also play the flute parts. But in the true spirit of music performance, the music will have more life, and will "breathe" better if two musicians are playing the pieces together live.

> *Guitarists of any skill level can use this book!*

The music covers a wide range of styles: Well-known classics include J.S Bach's "Jesu, Joy of Man's Desiring" and Claude Debussy's "Girl With the Flaxen Hair" (originally a solo piano piece). Lesser known, yet captivating pieces include a Mexican hat dance, a virtuoso Renaissance viola da gamba piece, and English guitar master John Renbourn's exquisite setting of the British ballad "The Trees They Do Grow High." There is even a jazzy version of "Greensleeves". Also included are several original compositions from the author. A full score for the quintet "Serenade in C" (included here as a duet) is available at www.Accent OnMusic.com.

The music was chosen partly for its beauty, and partly for its varying skill levels. For example, "Quant Je Voy Yver" will be very easy for both guitarists and flautists, while "The Trees They Do Grow High" and "Greensleeves 2" will challenge most players of both instruments.

The guitar part for every piece is written in several ways to accommodate players of all abilities. Standard notation is provided for classically trained guitarists who read. Tablature is provided for guitarists who prefer that medium. (A tablature guide appears on P. 47 of this book.) Also, each piece includes simplified chord names, along with a suggested strum and/or a simple fingerpicking pattern. In this way, less experienced guitarists can still provide adequate accompaniment for their flute partners, even if they can't play the written notes.

The Recording

The duet recording that accompanies this book is designed to accomplish a number of things. First, it allows the user to simply enjoy the duets from a listener's standpoint. Secondly, for guitarists who don't read notation, the recording facilitates learning the music by ear. Lastly, since the flute is panned to one side and the guitar to the other, it allows either of the instruments largely to be turned off so that an individual instrumentalist can use the recording as his/her playing "partner." There is a slight amount of "bleed" across tracks to allow the solo player to hear where his part is in relation to the other instrument.

> *For use by duos and by soloists!*

Also, a single instrumentalist can use the recording in a live performance if the sound system allows for amplification of one channel and not the other. To facilitate good "ensemble" playing—that is, staying together rhythmically—there is a simple rhythm track included when the "partner" track is not playing.

Table of Contents

CD Program

La Fille aux Cheveux de Lin

(Girl With the Flaxen Hair)

CD Track 2

Guitar: Standard Tuning

By Claude Debussy; Arrangement by Mark Hanson

•Easy Guitar: In this piece, simply strum first-position fingerings of the chords that are named. Since the guitar part does not use a steady rhythmic pattern, simply strum one downstoke for each chord listed.

Mexican Hat Dance

Guitar: Standard Tuning - Strummed*
Play each repeat at increased tempo:
Moderate - Faster - Fast

Traditional; Arrangement by Mark Hanson,
John Winbigler and Dave Ross

Guitar: Tacet first two measures

*Guitar strum
begins here

8va (Third Time Only)

(Pause before repeating)

Guitar:

Suggested Guitar Strums:

Traditional Arrangement © 2001 Mark D. Hanson

Foggy Dew

Guitar: Standard Tuning

Traditional; Arrangement by Mark Hanson

• **Easy Guitar:** Use first-position (end of the guitar neck) fingerings of the chords listed. This piece can be strummed with a simple down-up motion in 3/4 time. It also can be played with a repeating arpeggio fingerpicking pattern in 3/4 time, such as *p i m a m i* (T-I-M-R-M-I). Also, either eliminate the guitar solo on P. 9, or have the flute play the top line of the notated guitar solo.

"Foggy Dew"

(X = mute this string)

Jesu, Joy of Man's Desiring

Guitar: Standard Tuning

J.S. Bach; Arrangement by Mark Hanson

•**Easy Guitar:** Play first-position fingerings of the listed chords. **Strum:** Use a simple downstroke strum on each beat of each measure (three strums per measure). **Fingerpicking:** Simply pluck each listed chord on its appropriate beat(s) of each measure (three plucks per measure). **Flute:** Play the obligatto line (triplet eighth notes) whenever it appears in the guitar part (measures 12-13, for example).

Quant Je Voy Yver Retorner

(When I See Winter)

Guitar: Standard Tuning

Colin Muset; Arrangement by Mark Hanson

•**Easy Guitar:** The guitar accompaniment in this piece is the easiest one in the book. I hope that you can play it as written! The title is Old French, translated as "When I See Winter." This 13th-century piece is a musical description of the situation of professional musicians of the time – facing the approach of winter with little to sustain them.

Recercada Segunda

Guitar: Standard Tuning

Diego Ortiz; Arrangement by Mark Hanson

•**Easy Guitar:** The guitar part is an eight-measure phrase that repeats itself throughout the piece. A *very* steady rhythm is required of the guitarist, since the flute part is exceedingly rhythmic and is dependent on a steady rhythm in the accompaniment. **Strum:** A simple down-up in 3/4 time will work. **Fingerpicking:** Pluck the listed chords on each beat in 3/4 time, or in the notated rhythm.

"Recercada Segunda"

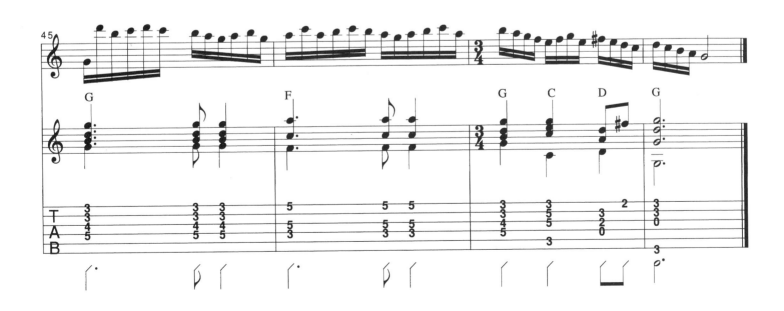

The Trees They Do Grow High

Guitar: Standard Tuning

Traditional; Arrangement by John Renbourn

•**Easy Guitar: Fingerpicking:** The best simplified fingerpicking pattern to use in "Trees" is the one Renbourn uses in measure 4, for example: *p i m/a i m/a i* (the middle and ring fingers pick their respective strings simultaneously). You may use a simpler arpeggio in 3/4 time: *p i m a m i*. The guitar part is simplified by using first-position fingerings of the notated chords, and by eliminating Renbourn's flourishes. **Strum:** Use a down-up pattern in 3/4 time on the listed chords.

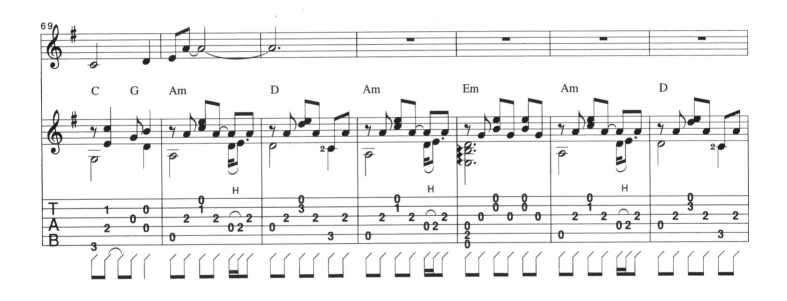

Em*: John Renbourn's actual fingering for measure 86 (notated to the right) will be quite challenging for most guitarists.

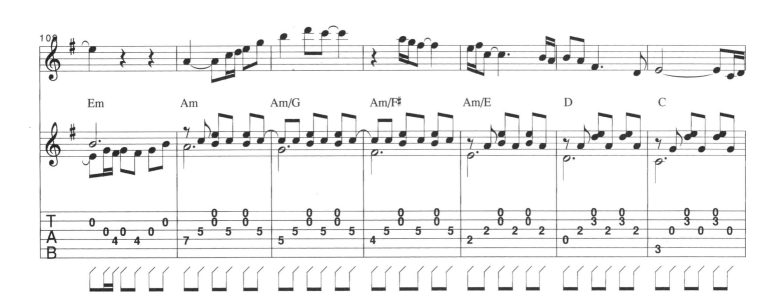

Golden Valley

Guitar: Standard Tuning

By Mark Hanson

•**Easy Guitar:** The flute and guitar play the melody together in "Golden Valley." **Strum:** Simply strum a down-up pattern in 4/4 time. **Fingerpicking:** A simple two-beat alternating-bass pattern (*p m p i*) will work, as will a simple arpeggio (*p i m a*). **Easy C#m7 fingering:** You may substitute a first-position Amaj7 fingering for the C#m7 chords (open first string; second string, 2nd fret; third string, 1st fret; fourth string, 2nd fret). Strum only the four treble strings.

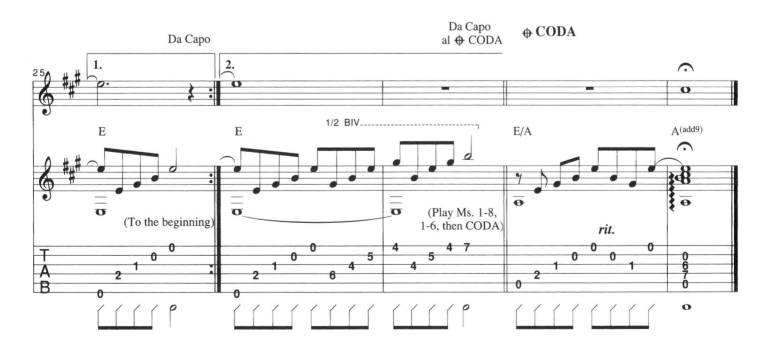

Serenade in C

Guitar: Standard Tuning

By Mark Hanson

•**Easy Guitar: Strum:** A simple down-up strum in 3/4 time will work nicely. **Fingerpicking:** Either the *p i m/a i m/a i* pattern or *p i m a m i* works. **Chords:** Do you best to learn the chords (for example: B-flat major7, Am with moving bass lines), since the harmony underlying a repeated melody is often what provides the continuing interest in this piece. "Serenade In C" was originally composed for guitar and flute/recorder quartet. The main melody is notated here for the flute. The full score is available through www.accentonmusic.com.

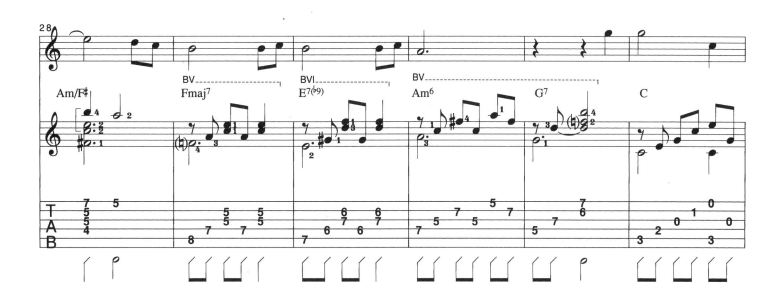

"Serenade in C"

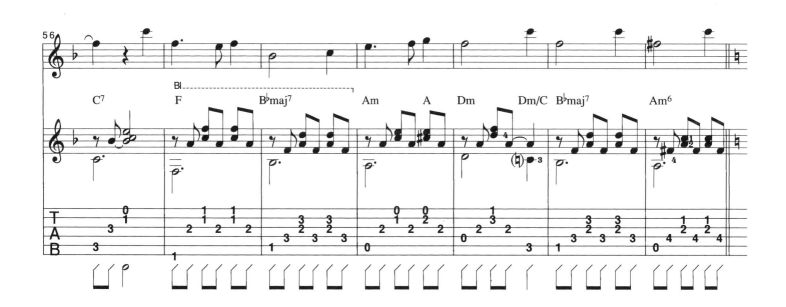

"Serenade in C"

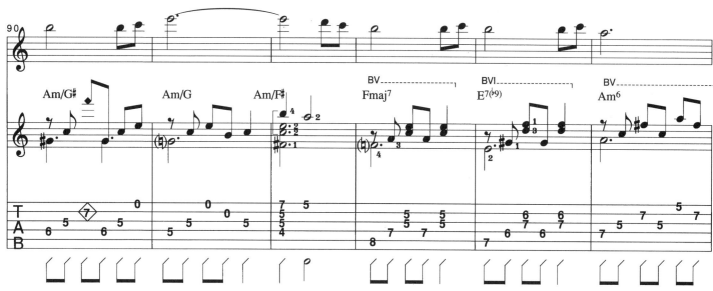

Ryan Time (Again)

Guitar: Drop-D Tuning (DAdgbe'), CAPO III

By Mark Hanson

•**Easy Guitar: Strum:** Use a down-up pattern for each beat. Please note that each beat in 12/8 and 9/8 time consists of *three* parts. Count each beat "1 & uh". Strum down on "1" and up on "uh". In doing so, you are strumming on the first and third subdivisions of each beat, providing the appropriate rhythm. In 12/8 measures you will strum down-up *four* times. In 9/8 measures you will strum down-up *three* times.
Fingerpicking: *p i m/a i* using the "1 & uh" rhythm, with *p* on "1" and *i* on "uh". You will play *p i m/a i* twice for 12/8, and *p i m/a i p i* for 9/8!

"Ryan Time (Again)"

Dear Reader: You are welcome to photocopy this page and attach it to P. 37 in order to avoid page turns.

Greensleeves 1

CD Track 12

Guitar: Standard Tuning

Traditional; Arrangement by Mark Hanson

•**Easy Guitar:** Play the notated chords at the end of the guitar neck. **Strum:** A single down strum for each notated chord on P. 39 is appropriate. On pages 40-41, a *down-up-up* eighth-note pattern (two times through the pattern for each measure) will work. **Fingerpicking:** On P. 39, pluck each chord once as notated. On pages 40-41, use a simple *p i m/a* (middle and ring fingers pick simultaneously on their respective strings) pattern. This is an eighth-note pattern, requiring two times through the pattern for each measure. **Flute:** Play the guitar melody on P. 40.

"Greensleeves 1"

Greensleeves 2
Jazz Improvisation

Faster, in 4

♩ = 136

•**Easy Guitar:** Except for measures 99-104 and 117-125, the guitar part of "Greensleeves 2" is a four-measure pattern that repeats many times. **Strum:** Until measure 117, a simple down-up strum in 4/4 time using the notated chords will suffice. From M. 117, simply strum each chord once with a downstroke. **Fingerpicking:** A simple two-beat arpeggio – *p i m/a i* or *p i m a* – will work. Better would be an eighth-note pattern with the following rhythmic emphasis: **1**-2-3-**1**-2-3-**1**-2-3-**1**-2-**1**-2. For instance: *p i m p i m p i m p i m p i p i*, with each thumb pluck emphasized.

"Greensleeves 2"

"Greensleeves 2"

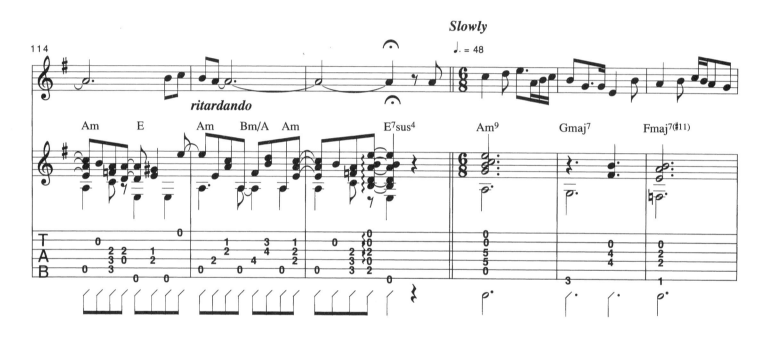

Tablature Guide

Tablature (TAB) is a notational system designed to show the instrumentalist at which fret to depress a string when plucking that string. Tablature has two main advantages over standard notation: 1) it indicates left-hand position, and 2) it is much easier to learn to read. Tablature also has its disadvantages, but for this book I recommend learning TAB if you don't read either.

Six horizontal lines represent the six strings of the guitar:

Treble:

A)

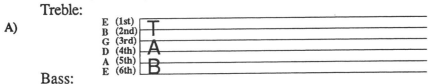

Bass:

A number on a line indicates at which fret to depress that string as you pluck it.

B)

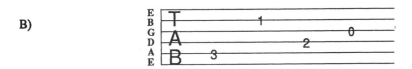

In Ex.B, a C-chord, you pluck the strings in this order:

1) fifth string fretted at the 3rd fret,
2) second string fretted at the 1st fret,
3) fourth string fretted at the 2nd fret,
4) third string open ("0" means an open string).

The stems and beams underneath the staff denote the rhythm:

C)

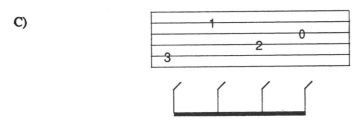

Ex. C contains four eighth notes, each receiving 1/2 beat in 2/4 time. To produce the correct rhythm, count evenly "1 & 2 &" with the notes as you pluck them.

Other rhythmic markings you will see include:

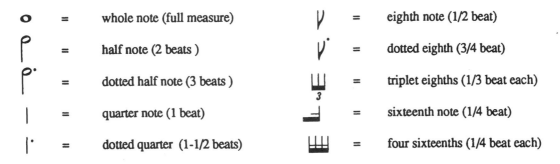

o	=	whole note (full measure)	♪	=	eighth note (1/2 beat)
♩	=	half note (2 beats)	♪·	=	dotted eighth (3/4 beat)
♩·	=	dotted half note (3 beats)	♫ (3)	=	triplet eighths (1/3 beat each)
|	=	quarter note (1 beat)		=	sixteenth note (1/4 beat)
|·	=	dotted quarter (1-1/2 beats)		=	four sixteenths (1/4 beat each)

"H" (Hammer-On), "P" (Pull-Off), and "S" (Slide) indicate notes articulated by the **left** hand.

Also from Accent On Music

- The Art of Contemporary Travis Picking
- The Art of Solo Fingerpicking
- Fingerstyle Blues Guitar Solos DVD
- The Complete Book of Alternate Tunings
- Alternate Tunings Picture Chords
- Masters of Hawaiian Slack Key Guitar
- Hymns and Spirituals for Fingerstyle Guitar
- Paul Simon Transcribed • Fingerstyle Noël
- The Music of Leo Kottke • Leo Kottke Transcribed
- Fingerstyle DVDs, Books, Recordings, TAB and much more

For more information, contact your local retailer.

Acknowledgements

I began arranging flute and guitar duets during college, many long years ago. At that time the repertoire ranged from Bach to pop, and folk to jazz. It still does!

The collection of music in this book represents my continuing interest in diverse genres of music. For the development of that interest and appreciation, I have many people to thank.

First, I would like to mention music professors Art Barnes and Leonard Ratner for helping me to understand how music works, and for exposing me to a vast world of music of which I knew little before coming under their tutelage.

I would like to thank my first flute partners: Cathy Meyer Frankowski, for showing me initially the possibilities of the flute and guitar combination; and Patty Farris Hennings, for demonstrating to me the beauty and joy a musician experiences performing in an ensemble. My thanks also go to Angela Owen, for providing a performance outlet for my early wind-instrument compositions.

My longtime flute partner Dave Ross deserves thanks for his friendship, luscious tone, and great musicianship. He also deserves credit for his willingness to play whatever I've written or arranged, and for encouraging me to write more.

Thanks also go to English guitar master John Renbourn for providing the stunning arrangement of "The Trees They Do Grow High," and to Pentangle Ltd. for granting us permission to reproduce it.

Kudos go to Chris Ledgerwood for another fantastic cover design. Thanks also go to James and Jean Goodall for the cover photo of their beautiful koa guitar; and to Collings Guitars for the mahogany SJ that I played on the recording.

As always, my deepest thanks go to my family for their enduring faith. Thanks also go to the folks at Music Sales in New York for their encouragement; to Patrick Mahoney, Jim Jasmin, and Jon Lindahl for computer and recording help; and to my friends at Pioneer Music, Gryphon Stringed Instruments, and Dusty Strings Music.

I hope you enjoy all of this!

Mark Hanson, October, 2001

About the Author

With music degrees from Stanford University, Mark Hanson and his wife Greta Pedersen currently own and operate Accent On Music LLC. Mark has authored over two dozen books and DVDs on varying aspects of guitar playing. He won a Grammy in 2005 for his contributions to the *Henry Mancini - Pink Guitar* CD. As an editor and columnist at *Frets* magazine, Mark interviewed such luminaries as James Taylor, David Crosby, Leo Kottke, John Renbourn, Roger McGuinn, and Michael Hedges. Mark's writings, arrangements and compositions appear regularly in a variety of guitar magazines. He also performs as a guitar soloist, with duet partners Greta Pedersen and Doug Smith, and as a member of Acoustic Guitar Summit. Mark has shared the stage with such well-known guitarists as Renbourn, Tommy Emmanuel, Laurence Juber, Ed Gerhard, and the late Jerry Garcia. Each summer Mark and Greta host the annual Accent On Music Guitar Seminar in Portland, Ore. To see what other publications Mark has authored, please visit your local retailer, or visit **www.AccentOn Music.com.**